SUMMARY

How often have we known wonderful single people that never seem to find a satisfying relationship?

Married people are one of two things, Very Happy or Very Unhappy. Why does such a vast disparity exist?

"Establishing Glory: The Relationship Handbook" answers many of these questions by taking us on a journey from being single and learning ourselves through dating to marriage and back to being single again, all from a Christian man's perspective.

Through this journey, you will see an uncut level of truth that many men feel but aren't willing to share.

ESTABLISHING GLORY 2

ESTABLISHING GLORY 2

The Relationship Handbook

JACKIE SMITH, JR.

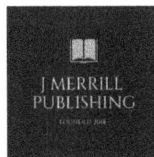

J MERRILL
PUBLISHING

ISBN: 978-1-950719-05-1 (Hardback)
ISBN: 978-1-950719-03-7 (Paperback)
ISBN: 978-1-950719-04-4 (eBook)

Library of Congress Control Number: 2019904500

Any references to historical events, real people, or real places are used fictitiously. Names, characters, and places are products of the author's imagination.

Second printing edition 2019.

J Merrill Publishing, Inc.
434 Hillpine Drive
Columbus, OH 43207

www.JMerrillPublishingInc.com

CONTENTS

PREFACE

The purpose of this book is to provide balance. I grew up as a young man in the 1970s in the United States, specifically in Ohio, in a two-parent home and a church. I've learned that people yearn for relationships, yet nobody, especially the church, addresses what that means.

The church taught us we couldn't love one another successfully until we learned to love God. To this, I wholeheartedly agree. However, can anyone tell me how to love God? What does it mean to be in a relationship with Him? How does divine love and relationship translate to being in a relationship with a woman?

For years, I was confounded by that analogy. When I see an attractive woman in yoga pants, my thoughts aren't on God but on how to get closer to her.

Oh, wait—I forgot to mention something. If you have read my first book, *"Establishing Glory: The Praise and Worship Handbook,"* understand that this book is not an extension of that.

One issue today is the refusal to be authentic in our lives. We have been coaxed into adopting an approach marked by political correctness, reticent grace, and accepting "that's just how the world is" philosophies.

As stated in the first line of this book, the aim is to provide balance.

The unsettling reality is that when we go to church, we don't hear about relationships, sex, and sexuality until a high-profile televangelist is caught cheating, someone is accused of molestation, or we notice openly gay individuals participating in the choir or band.

My question is, why?

If sex and sexuality are among the most pressing challenges that people—not just the church—face, then why isn't the church more consistent in its message and stance on these subjects?

It's easy to criticize Bishop Eddie L. Long for his history of child molestation, sexual misconduct, and homosexuality. However, similar issues are rampant worldwide in the Catholic Church! Who is consistently teaching us that this is the wrong path? Who is sounding the alarm that God is displeased? Who is discussing these issues with our children?

If we can't have an open dialogue about relationships, sex, and sexuality among adults, how can we extend this conversation to the next generation? We aren't having these conversations with our children.

Our children are learning from our silence and YouTube videos. They converse about these topics while playing video games and are influenced by a curriculum that promotes alternative lifestyles, all while we remain silent for fear of offending.

So where is the balance?

In the past, we had church mothers and deacons who, in their own way, taught us to be men and women of standard, unashamed of it. Time has passed, and those mentors are gone. We are the ones who need to uphold those standards and guide the next generation, yet we are losing them because we're too focused on imitating their lifestyle.

That's why I'm writing this book.

If you're easily offended by real talk, I apologize in advance.

❧ I ❧
SINGLE AND SATISFIED

"You complete me." "My better half." These are phrases that imply imperfection, insufficiency, and, quite honestly, defectiveness.

To discuss relationships with others, we first must explore the relationship with ourselves. Understanding who you are encompasses your desires, needs, ambitions, drive, triggers, and what you dislike, don't need, or don't want.

Relationships become complex because we create ever-changing rules. The goalposts keep shifting.

In my youth, I had an insatiable thirst for life. I loved simply doing something— anything. As a church-going kid, I attended most services and had a rich social life outside the church. I loved God, and I cherished the diversity of His creation.

I found a balance in my life early on. While I did date, I was a late bloomer by today's standards, becoming sexually active around the ages of sixteen or seventeen. So, spending time with friends didn't imply sexual activity, though it happened occasionally.

My focus was on life itself—free from the constraints of dating, relationships, or societal rules.

Then came the United States Air Force. I was slated for deployment to Desert Storm but got injured during Security Police training. I ended up at Yokota Air Base in Tokyo, Japan, for over two years, where I had a myriad of experiences that shook my world.

Imagine a twenty-one-year-old, reasonably handsome churchgoer dropped in the middle of the "Land of the Rising Sun." When I received my orders, my mother, an open-minded individual, warned me against bringing home a Japanese woman. Her comment shook me to my core.

In Japan, my focus initially remained on work, church, and maintaining relationships with African American women. However, the latter became increasingly challenging, as many had reservations because of the behaviors of other servicemen.

Navigating this complex social landscape, I engaged in short-term relationships with Japanese nationals. Interestingly, these relationships were mutually understood to be temporary, keeping things straightforward.

But sex doesn't equate to happiness. Eventually, even in Japan, I craved solitude over the company of multiple women. I found solace in being single and content with my own being, free from external validation.

One of the most significant challenges people face is internal—self-esteem, self-confidence, and self-validation. If you're struggling with yourself, how can you be a fulfilling partner to someone else? As my pastor used to say, "It's a poor frog that won't croak in his own pond."

To genuinely embrace singlehood, we must first be content and satisfied with ourselves. What obstacles are you facing that prevent you from being genuinely single and satisfied? And what needs to happen for you to overcome those obstacles?

❦ 2 ❦

WHO ARE YOU

One of the most complicated questions to answer concerns identity. All too often, we succumb to generalizations, categorizations, and classifications based on gender, age, ethnicity, religion, socioeconomics, creed, and color. But none of this can genuinely answer the fundamental question: Who are you?

I am an African American, middle-class man in my late forties living in the Midwest. I work every day at a Fortune 100 company, live in a decent home, pay bills and taxes, attend church every week, and consider myself a good and kind person.

These attributes describe aspects of who I am, but they don't answer the question. Who you are isn't determined by what you have; it's defined by how you think. The Bible says in Proverbs 23:7 (NKJV), *"For as he thinks in his heart, so is he."*

The items on the list help to describe how I think, but those are merely things. In relationships, I must genuinely know who I am to be the best me I can be. Once I'm in touch with who I am, I can accommodate you.

A common issue is that women are with you, but aim to mold you into someone else, their ideal man. This is evident when women talk about how they will change their men. It tells me that his identity isn't set. Soft clay is pliable; once hardened, it can only be broken.

This divergence leads to conflict. She wants one thing, but he's not that. She's trying to "break" him. Men often say, "She's just tripping." No, bro; she's trying to break a wild stallion—a stallion unaware that he's wild.

So, how do we begin the journey of self-actualization?

As a Christian man, my first answer is always to ask God. Through a journey with God, He can answer these questions for you. Matthew 7:7 (NIV) advises, *"Ask and it will be given to you; seek and you will find; knock and the door will be opened to you."*

But not everyone reading this book is on a faith journey.

According to Maslow's Hierarchy of Needs[1], the journey begins with basic needs like food, water, warmth, and rest. Then comes safety and security. These form the foundation upon which we build psychological needs like belonging and esteem. Finally, we enter into self-fulfillment needs, including self-actualization.

I say all this to make a point: it's a process. When we truly begin to love ourselves, we take the time to understand ourselves.

It's a sad state of affairs when men's only association with themselves is media representation. As a Black man, I must be an athlete, an artist, or some sort of gangster to be deemed extraordinary. Why? Because that's how we're portrayed in the media.

LeBron James is larger than life—an athlete.

Kevin Hart is larger than life—an artist.

Snoop Dogg is larger than life—an artist and gangster.

For years, I aspired to be what I saw in the media, but I didn't fit the mold. I started looking within and found myself. I discovered that I love writing, playing musical instruments, spending time in nature, and seeking truth. I love handholding, hugs, kisses, and undivided attention. All these are things I learned about myself, separate from any external influence.

So, what makes you unique?

What do you love about yourself?

What do you love?

༃ 3 ༃

WHAT DO YOU WANT

The title of this chapter poses a trick question because there is no definitive answer. To clarify, I think the question should be, "What do you want today?"

As we mature, our perspectives and desires evolve. Earlier in life, I was thrilled at the prospect of getting my diaper changed. As I grew, my focus shifted to gaining throwback Chuck Taylors or Air Jordans. The same evolution applies to our relational desires.

During my late teens and early twenties, I dated several young women. I didn't realize it then, but I had established a pattern. I specifically remember Ava, a young woman who stood out for two reasons: she was an excellent cook and loved intimacy.

My mother noticed Ava didn't fit the mold of the women I'd previously dated. Naturally, she questioned my interest in her. And being the dutiful son that I was, I evaded the truth. The real reason I spent time with Ava was her ease of intimacy—followed by a satisfying meal.

This focus on Ava came at the expense of my relationship with Madison, a woman who genuinely loved me. Madison was reserved and self-respectful. In hindsight, I should have focused on building a future with her rather than chasing after Ava, a fleeting pleasure.

As men mature, so do our desires. In the early 1990s, I wanted different things than I did in 2018. Therefore, the answer to what one truly desires isn't constant; it changes as we evolve.

Here's an exercise: List what you don't want in your relationship. Here are a few things I absolutely don't want:

- A man. In today's society, clarity is paramount. I believe in heterosexual relationships.
- A weak woman. A relationship is a partnership; there's no room for dominance and submissiveness.
- A religious woman. Being scrupulously faithful isn't the same as showing evidence of godly fruit or communion.

As you compile your list, your preferences will become clear. Remember, your desires will evolve, so this exercise requires immediate application to avoid being held hostage by emotional shifts.

Take your time on this exercise. When you're purposeful in your steps forward, you can expect more favorable results. Trust me, there are few things worse than realizing you've moved in the wrong direction—I speak from experience.

❧ 4 ❧
DATING

I'm the first to admit that I don't have all the answers, but I will find them.

Since I had been married to my ex-wife for over twenty-two years, I wasn't prepared for the dating scene. Why? Because in the late 1990s, people were different, expectations were different, and, quite honestly, everything was different.

So, as an analyst, I did what I knew: I conducted tests.

LET'S DO LUNCH

For close to a year, I took time to learn what women in the 2010s were looking for, what they wanted, and where their heads were regarding dating, relationships, and men in general. I started going out to lunch with the women from my job. To be fair and balanced, I went on a lot of lunches with a wide variety of women.

During these lunches, we visited several restaurants around the job—from Chipotle to Max & Erma's, from Chinese to Greek, from food courts to fine dining. Sometimes, I paid; sometimes, we split the bill. But the key to these lunches was that there were no preconceived notions that these were dates or preludes to some intimate relationship. These were meals with friends.

One thing everyone knew was that I was dealing with divorce and that I wasn't interested in kindling any new flames. Other than that, the gloves were off.

Most of the time, once we sat down, I didn't have to say much at all.

Fellas: Women love to talk. So, if you want to know something about them, allow them to be themselves. You'll learn everything you need to know!

Again, most times, I didn't have to say much at all.

I had lunch with Charlotte. I asked, "Hey, how are things going with you?"

When these words floated from my mouth, I found out her current living situation, relationship status, random things about her family, how much money certain people owed her, who her friends were, who hated her, and how many men she was currently sleeping with. But wait—I learned all of this in less than forty-five minutes!

I went to lunch with Sofia and asked a similar icebreaker question.

I learned she was reserved regarding men because she had been hurt several times. She didn't like being single, but the surrounding options were limited. She was content taking care of her teenage child. Another thing about her was that she was dealing with some genuine health concerns. When she had flare-ups, it wasn't pretty. And, finally, the guy she was seeing was not being a man of his word and was being a plain old jerk.

Then there was Chloe.

Chloe was cool. She was reluctant even to have lunch because "she didn't do that kind of thing." But we did, and I learned about the difficulty of single-parenting and raising two children. She loved talking about her dreams. She wanted to live on a particular side of town, in a specific type of house, with a certain number of bedrooms and bathrooms. And I can't forget: IKEA would fully furnish the home. What made Chloe cool was not only that she was a dreamer, but also a hard worker. She worked toward attaining those dreams. The guy she was dating was mistreating her children.

After only a few lunches, I saw a theme.

These women were crazy!

But they were crazy for a reason. The men in their lives weren't good. Each of these women had a history of men problems. Each settled for their guy, and the guy knew she was settling.

The good part for the latter two women is that they moved on from the uncool situations. Thank God!

Now, I can't wholly blame the men, though. Women also have roles to play in these foul situations. Like, if a man is mistreating your children, he needs to go. You managed your bills and home before he moved into your place. So, forget the financial gain he brings; for the sake of the children, he needs to be evicted, at a minimum.

The good thing about these lunches is that not every woman I shared the table with was a basket case.

Victoria was amazing. She was a fitness consultant with Weight Watchers who had lost over two hundred pounds, if I remember correctly. She loved running and frequently took part in various marathons. She is a happily married woman, and the love of her life is her grandson, whom we'll call Andrew.

Andrew is genuinely her love. I smile, even now, thinking about all the Andrew stories and pictures she shared.

One thing Victoria recommended was that

I take a vacation to Jamaica before getting into another meaningful relationship. The reason is that when she completed her divorce, she took that vacation, and it did her a world of good. She wasn't Stella but was released from the bondage of her past during this trip.

Moving on to Hannah... She was a beautiful, intelligent, God-fearing woman who knew what she wanted, where she wanted to be, and had a plan to get there. When we first went to lunch, she focused on work and raising her child. Our lunch was refreshing; we spoke on an intellectual level, comparing thoughts about church, God's role in people's lives, and fulfilling one's destiny. The most remarkable thing about her was that, as time passed, a gentleman found her, and they eventually married.

We must never forget that there are several "someones" out there for everyone. We often don't meet these unique individuals because we don't make ourselves accessible; we live in a bubble.

I grew up in a family church where I was related to everyone. Consequently, the only time I met any eligible young women was when other churches visited or when we visited other churches. Could I expect to meet my future spouse at my family church? It's possible, but maybe I need to broaden my horizons.

⟡

WOULD YOU LIKE TO HANG OUT SOMETIME?

There are several reasons people date: one, sex; two, appearance; three, companionship; four, all of the above.

Let's Talk about Hooking Up

How often have you heard the phrase "We all have our needs"? In such cases, the speaker is usually justifying their sexual activities. Sometimes we hook up with people we'd never otherwise consider, fueled by either lust or the simple passage of time since our "last time."

My first roommate in Japan was indifferent about whom he slept with. Any woman who paid him the slightest attention was fair game. As his roommate, I had to endure his late-night escapades.

Hooking up often leads to emotional damage. Emotions get involved, and someone ends up getting hurt. Take Felicia, for example. She loved to cook and often sent plates my way. One day, I arrived to find her answering the door in nothing but a T-shirt. I was faced with a moral dilemma, and, regrettably, my baser instincts won. I stayed for dinner—and dessert.

Appearance Over Substance

Have you ever heard statements like, "Honey, you're not getting any younger. You need to find somebody"? Sometimes, people date to keep others off their backs.

In Hollywood, for instance, a handsome

man might be seen with a beautiful woman one day and another the next. Eventually, we discover he's gay.

Then there was Aria. I loved hanging out with her, not because sex was the objective, but because we genuinely enjoyed each other's company. She liked the appearance of having a man in her life but didn't want the commitment that came with it.

The Search for Companionship

"It is not good that the man should be alone" (Genesis 2:18, King James Version). Companionship requires mutual goals and intentions.

Take Monica, for instance. We met in the cereal aisle at Kroger and talked for nearly ninety minutes. Although we enjoyed each other's company, we eventually discovered that we were too similar for a romantic relationship.

When companionship is the goal, life becomes more evident. You're not concerned with what others think or jumping into bed; you're focused on building a relationship. Option four is the perfect combination: I reconnected with a lifelong friend and found an excellent addition to my life.

So, what are your reasons for dating a particular person? What makes you dateable?

5

HE THAT FINDETH...

For just a moment, I want to speak to the men.

Until now, it has been all fun and games. We've learned a bit about the single life and some of its aspects—understanding ourselves and navigating the dating scene. We've experienced both success and failure. However, when it all boils down, the immediate impact involves only two people: her and me.

This is the point at which we need to elevate our game. We're in the big leagues now. No more child's play; this is serious business.

The first question to ask is, "What are you looking for?"

> "He that findeth a wife findeth
> a good thing, and obtaineth
> favour of the LORD,"
>
> — (PROVERBS 18:22, KJV)

Finding a woman is easy. In the United States, women make up more than half of the population. So, sheer numbers show that there are many options if you're looking for a woman. Women come in all shapes, sizes, ages, economic backgrounds, and education levels. This array might seem like a buffet at first glance.

However, a real man is not just looking for a woman; he's searching for a wife. Proverbs 31:10 declares, *"Who can find a virtuous woman? for her price is far above rubies"* (KJV).

A man with proper self-esteem will

recognize the value that a good wife adds to his life.

Now, let's shift the focus to the ladies.

If you've had enough of casual and temporary relationships and yearn for something more enduring, know that God places high value on you. He directs your future husband to build a relationship that mirrors this divine view.

Proverbs 31:10 reiterates, *"Who can find a virtuous woman? for her price is far above rubies."* The man who becomes your husband should see your worth, not merely his perception of your value to him. He should love you *"as Christ also loved the church, and gave himself for it"* (Ephesians 5:25, KJV).

This image is not of a man who merely provides financial security and a place to live. While men like that abound, many are so self-centered that they desire a spouse who will focus solely on them. Such an environment will starve you of the affection that fosters growth.

In Ephesians 5, the Bible speaks of mutual submission within marriage. Marriage is not a

50-50 arrangement: it's 100-100. As God loves His church, so should you be loved. As the Church reflects God's grace, so should you, as a priceless pearl, illuminate your husband's life.

Strength and power come from being this priceless pearl. If your husband hasn't yet discovered his divine role, your commitment to God can guide him toward *"a life of real love"* (1 Corinthians 7:13–14, KJV).

However, those same verses clarify that if an unbelieving spouse is unwilling to stay in the relationship without causing harm, this is unacceptable. Such a circumstance is not life together but mere cohabitation; you must not endure such abuse.

The key to your happiness lies first in self-respect and then in bestowing that respect upon others. If you struggle with poor self-esteem, begin with your mindset. As mentioned earlier, as you think, so you shall become.

This is a message to both men and women.

One simple thing I learned while having

those lunches is that when a man shows genuine interest, even partially, a woman can quickly become a candidate for a long-term relationship.

Women are tired of sorry men. They're frustrated with the games, the lying, the cheating, and the misrepresentations. Women are done with it!

Some have chosen to become players, like the men who hurt them. Others are choosing alternative lifestyles, assuming they can avoid the heartbreak they've experienced, only to discover that unhealthy relationships come from all directions.

Finally, many women respond to men by isolating themselves. This response is incredibly hurtful to me. So many outstanding women have chosen 'nothing' to avoid the potential pain of being in a relationship. I know a woman who wanted this life and still ended up being stalked, her home broken into, and almost raped—each event by different men.

To be more than honest, my heart goes out to women. You are incredible creatures!

There's nothing on this earth more amazing than a woman! And this is one reason I drafted this book.

Some might compare our search for the right husband or wife to being a coal miner. Coal is plentiful and accessible. But without it, there's a lot we would not enjoy.

But let me be clear: I'm not a coal miner but a diamond miner.

Diamonds are more precious than coal. They've been formed under extreme temperatures and pressures. Diamonds have taken the most challenging situations and transformed into something of greater value. The diamonds that can best complement our lives are those that have not just reacted to life but have responded to it.

When searching for a diamond, I look for the Four Cs: cut, color, clarity, and carat weight. These are the essential elements of any diamond. Let me explain.

CUT

The first thing any man or woman notices is what they can see. The "cut" refers to someone's appearance: Is it pleasing to the eye? Is there a special glimmer in their eyes?

Men are visual, and women know this. So, don't be fooled. When she puts on those yoga pants, she knows we're going to look. She was aware we were paying attention when she wore that dress and high heels.

Women are visual, too. They notice the guy who knows his way around a gym and has that chiseled look. But they are also watching for character and inner strength.

When men wear trendy business suits or the latest hip-hop outfits, they know they will not go unnoticed. They may adopt an attitude, hoping to catch the ladies' eyes.

Just like women, men can't help but advertise. Both are shoppers, and both expect to be shopped.

If you know what Christian Louboutin is, you know everyone is looking for that one person who has "the cut."

Every Thursday, I go to lunch with my all-male team. One of the recurring conversations is about the women who pass by our table or the window outside the restaurant.

And when women get together for coffee, they watch the parade of guys passing by.

Everyone can't help but notice those who appear to have it "all together."

COLOR

One promise I've made to myself is always to be honest when I write.

We humans can be very racist. We Black people can be even more racist than any other group. Why? Because we exhibit racist tendencies within our own race.

I am a dark-skinned Black man. Growing up in the 1970s, being dark-skinned was unpopular. Over the years, I've had to overcome the stereotypes placed on me because of my skin color. The name-calling and teasing—Blackie Jackie, Blackjack—were painful periods in my life. Worse, I perpetuated that pain onto others.

For many years, I wouldn't give a second glance at a dark-skinned Black woman. Despite her beauty, her skin tone was a turnoff. I'd use phrases like, "She's cute, but two dark-skinned people can't get together. The kids will come out blurple." I projected my insecurities onto others who felt the same pain.

Consequently, I gravitated toward women who were brown-skinned, red-boned, or high-yellow. I avoided women of other races and ethnicities.

But one day, I broke the color barrier and hung out with a mixed-race young woman—Black and Japanese. From that day forward, I was a free man.

We all have preferences for diamond colors: pink, blue, white, or even chocolate. Preferences need not become prejudices. Yet, when it comes to skin color, prejudices can be not only real but also limiting.

CLARITY

Clarity focuses on the psyche of the diamonds around us.

Picture this: someone who looks striking enters the room. Everyone notices she is dynamite or that he's a real hunk. Miss Dynamite opens her mouth, or Mr. Hunk speaks up, and the dumbest things are released into the air.

Simply stated, water seeks its own level.

I'm not a street guy, so a "hood chick" wouldn't be a fit for me; there are certain things that I don't think about or perceive.

A woman who is not a sports fan wouldn't be a good fit for the handsome jock at the center of the room.

Now, I am a thinker. So, someone who can engage my thoughts is a good fit.

I am an educated man, so someone with a particular level of education or thought is a good fit.

I love God and family, so someone who genuinely loves God and family is an excellent fit for me.

Clarity is also about speaking the same language. We often fall for the package. She's extraordinarily attractive; she can cook and is excellent in bed. Or he's a gentleman and drives a sports car. But those things are shallow.

There are over 125 million women in the United States. At least half of them are attractive, can cook, and can satisfy your sexual urges—but can you have a meaningful conversation with her? There are men everywhere with fancy cars and a certain attractive suaveness, but can the conversation go beyond him or his vehicle?

Clarity is crucial because the mind will last long after looks have faded.

CARAT WEIGHT

Carat weight is character. I could complete this entire book just by defining this one quality.

According to Merriam-Webster, character is:

- One of the attributes or features that make up and distinguish an individual
- The complex of mental and ethical traits marking and often individualizing a person, group, or nation
- Moral excellence and firmness

In short, character is who you are when no one is looking. It's what separates and distinguishes you from everyone else. It's the mark of a diamond.

A person's character can and will be displayed in many ways.

I had a conversation with my friend about the fact that I don't open the car door for her. After I proposed, she told her father I didn't open the car door for her. Naturally, as a father, he wanted to know why.

My answer was straightforward and true to my character: "Her hands aren't broken."

That is me. If I suddenly started opening the car door for her, I wouldn't be true to myself. I would be trying to be someone else, which I don't do.

When we're together, she never has to worry about being cared for. There's nothing I don't offer or do within my means. That's my character.

Character also encompasses expectations, wants, wishes, and desires. Notice that needs are not a part of character but a separate subject altogether.

Since character deals with mentality and ethics, expectations differ from person to person. For some, the expectation of opening the car door might be a deal-breaker because they view it as a sign of disrespect or lack of courtesy. Others might see it as condescending or a slight against femininity and equality.

The thing to remember about finding a spouse is that it's a choice. While we might be diamond miners, we see many diamonds. The task we all face is deciding which diamond to stick with.

This is my third marriage. Before I got married the first time, there were several candidates; the same was true before this marriage.

I had to make a choice: which diamond would be mine? But how do you distinguish one diamond from another?

✺ 6 ✺

CELIBACY

Celibacy: "The state of abstaining from marriage and sexual relations." **Translation:** Keep your stuff to yourself.
Any questions?

❦

Itried to leave this topic out, but I couldn't resist. Celibacy and abstinence are touchy subjects, both figuratively and literally. Abstinence represents temporary avoidance of sex, whereas celibacy is a lifestyle.

As you may have noticed in previous chapters, I haven't been a shining example of either. I could easily rely on the rhetoric that says, "I'm a man, and I need to get some," or "The spirit indeed is willing, but the flesh is weak" (Matthew 26:41, KJV). However, I won't.

The reason I can write this book is that I have experienced everything about which I write. This book serves as a cleansing process for me. I've had sex outside of marriage multiple times with various women. When they weren't around, I engaged in solo sexual activities (more on that shortly).

I take full responsibility for my sexual escapades. The devil didn't make me do it. Though he may have played a role, quite honestly, I wanted it each time. Here's the deal: Once certain doors open, only an act of God can close them. However, God doesn't close doors we wish to remain open.

I've abstained from sex when it was convenient. When between relationships, I didn't always desire the whole dinner-movie-sex routine. I was uncertain whether I wanted to engage in the conversations that came before and after sex. There were also times when I earnestly sought God and didn't want to be distracted.

There were reasons I abstained. But remember, abstinence is temporary.

I know a woman—let's call her Mary—who lives a celibate lifestyle. Mary isn't who you'd expect to be celibate. She's not a shy, homely woman wearing sackcloth. Quite the contrary, Mary is attractive and lively. She is reserved in her dress, but she is no slouch. She doesn't advertise because she's not selling. Her home revolves around her faith in God. She mostly watches faith-based or family-oriented television.

Some might think Mary is boring, but she is anything but. She knows what she wants and creates an environment that is controlled. Last I heard, she had been celibate for over ten years, and for that, I applaud her.

When I was single, my environment wasn't as virtuous. I was a free spirit and dressed accordingly. I leaned toward business-casual attire but suited up when necessary. My TV watching was eclectic, ranging from horror movies to cartoons to pornography.

Quick pause: Be honest—what does your TV-viewing habit say about you?

My viewing choices reflected my lifestyle. I sought thrills, loved to laugh, and, frankly, loved sex.

Let's get real: Seeking sex with multiple partners is defined as "being a hoe" in the Urban Dictionary. The term refers to someone who sleeps with multiple people simultaneously, thinking that's okay.

Let's explore why this isn't good.

PHYSICAL HEALTH

It's called disease. According to the CDC,

> "Breaking news from the 2018 National STD Prevention Conference: New CDC data find that nearly 2.3 million cases of chlamydia, gonorrhea, and syphilis were diagnosed in the United States in 2017. Public health leaders, including those from the Association of State and Territorial Health Officials (ASTHO), National Coalition of STD Directors (NCSD), and the University of Alabama's School of Medicine, join CDC onsite to discuss the new findings and how to counter the country's STD epidemic."
>
> — (AUGUST 28, 2018)

There are 2.3 million cases of chlamydia, gonorrhea, and syphilis. However, this number does not include herpes, HIV, and AIDS.

I was recently listening to a radio show, and one of the co-hosts said, "After I've gone through six or seven condoms, then I'm going raw; because by then, we've established trust between each other." What?

Keep in mind, he said, "six or seven condoms." In a subsequent statement, he clarified that these might be used during six or seven visits or six or seven times in one visit. How in the world are you establishing trust?

No, sir. You are rolling the dice with your life.

My thinking regarding condom use was solely based on the individual's history. Why? Because I was not too fond of condoms. While "interviewing" the candidate, I listened for critical phrases regarding abstinence—e.g., "It's been a year since I've had sex," or "I haven't been with anyone since 2016."

Considering my health, I judged a woman's suitability as a sexual partner based on the time since she last had sex. I knew I was healthy—I had been tested, and my results were clear.

However, how many of us know that people lie?

Just as I was interviewing candidates, they

were interviewing me. And people are proficient at telling their version of a story.

Having sex, for some people, only means vaginal penetration. They don't count oral or anal sex, nor the multiple people they've kissed. Many diseases are transmitted through bodily fluids, such as saliva. And then you wonder why you have sores in your mouth.

Let's move on.

MENTAL / SPIRITUAL HEALTH

"The mind is a terrible thing to waste" is often said in the context of education, but it's also true concerning relationships. If my aim was a one-night stand, once I achieved that, I moved on. The thrill was in the chase, and the excitement was in the conquest.

I know a notably abstinent woman. She had a knack for crushing a man's spirit by rejecting his advances. We became friends and shared a lot. Initially, I was interested in her, mainly for sexual reasons, but we connected on a deeper level. The problem was I was also involved with another woman, complicating my emotional and spiritual state.

These connections are called "soul ties." They don't just vanish—you must be cleansed and delivered from them.

Pornography is another issue. Jeremiah 17:9 (KJV) says, *"The heart is deceitful above all things, and desperately wicked: who can know it?"* Pornography is addictive and, left unchecked, can lead you down a dark path. If you find yourself in such a place, seek licensed counseling and spiritual guidance.

We risk more than just a good time when we fail to practice abstinence or celibacy. Our very lives and souls are at stake.

I don't have specific questions at the end of this chapter. However, I'd like you to ponder your sexual choices and the potential consequences.

For more information on STDs, visit <u>the CDC's website</u>.

✼ 7 ✼

THE BIG DAY

Just for the fellas, the "big day" is the Wedding Day—the day your lady has been waiting for since she was born.

Young girls dream about finding their Prince Charming, being swept off their feet, and being carried away by the man of their dreams.

Since this is already their mindset, one of the best pieces of advice I can offer is to keep your head down, agree to everything, and smile.

The end!

Now, if you believe any of those opening paragraphs, then keep reading for the actual story.

We've been trained to believe that the day a man and woman get married is "Her Day." We see wedding shows like "Say Yes to the Dress," "Bridezillas," and "Married at First Sight." Then we have movies like "My Best Friend's Wedding," "Runaway Bride," and "My Big Fat Greek Wedding." Everything we see points us in the direction that it's all about the woman.

But that kind of thinking is totally out of balance. The marriage relationship is a moment that is shared. Is it a special moment for the bride? Yes. She expected that this would be the pinnacle of her life, and it is, even without the hype of social and cultural media. But the groom also experiences a special moment. His life is changing. This time is to be equally shared between the two of them and less as a fairy-tale social occasion for the entertainment of others.

After all, without each other, where would they be?

Quick answer? Single.

Everything from the proposal to the honeymoon is about the two becoming one. It's about us.

THE PROPOSAL

It's every woman's dream to be loved and have that love sealed with that romantic moment of the proposal. And every man faces the possibility that this anticipated moment might not have a happy ending.

We know how this works. We're out to dinner at our favorite restaurant. We had a fantastic time. The service was excellent. The food was terrific. And the conversation was pleasant, as usual.

And then, the couple's favorite song is playing out of the blue? The guy gets all nervous. His throat is suddenly dry, and he can barely speak. She watches as he reaches into his pocket and pulls out a little box. He stands up, only long enough to get down on one knee.

She is watching his lips move and realizes that words are coming out of his mouth that sound like, "Will you marry me?"

The universe explodes because this is the pivotal moment in life. People celebrate. The screams of excitement fill the air. And everything in life pauses for a moment, waiting for her answer.

Then, there it is: "Yes." And the cheering begins all over again.

We might be tempted to think the "yes" is the most significant moment. Still, in all the celebrations, we quickly forget that another feature of the event is just as pivotal: the moment this guy risks it all by asking in the first place.

Now, both of them have made a life-changing decision. They have committed to a life with each other and with no one else. The other suitors are history. The flings are over. Both have turned in their playing card and taken themselves off the market. In the words of Michael Jackson, "This is it!"

This decision is not a light one. It solidifies your choice to be with one woman. When I proposed to my wife, the part in the vows that says, "Forsaking all others," flashed like breaking news before my eyes. It was a reminder and a warning.

But I am not a hopeless romantic. My proposal went something like this. My friend called me. She was going to the emergency room because she was experiencing a lot of pain. It was around 7 a.m.

So, I contacted my job to inform them I'd be late because my friend was in the ER.

I proceeded to the hospital to be by her side because I hated seeing someone in the ER alone. It's bad enough that they are there, but to be there without support isn't cool to me.

When I arrived, the medical staff was doing their thing: running tests, taking her blood pressure, and so forth. The doctor had been in the room to tell us what was happening and to set our expectations.

Quick note: Notice how I switched from going to see her to how the doctor was talking to us.

As often happens in the ER, we were left in the room for a long time. The TV was on, but we weren't watching it. Every so often, we'd update the family with our current status.

Then, suddenly, I heard someone talking— and it was me.

Me: "Do you want to go ahead and do this?"

Her: "Sure."

Me: "When?"

Her: "Don't play, Jackie."

Me: "Okay, let's start over. Do you really want to go ahead and do this? Yes or no because I don't know what 'sure' means."

Her: "Yes," (long pause) "as long as you're not playing."

Me: "Okay, cool. I don't have the ring right now. We can get it later. And I'm sorry, but I'm not getting on this dirty floor."

Her: "Okay." (Pauses) "Are you really serious?"

I then pulled out my cell phone and texted our immediate families. About an hour later, I went through my contacts and sent a message to every woman with whom I was close, hanging out, friends, had any feelings for, and any woman my new fiancée had a problem with. I let them know individually that I'd just proposed, and she said yes.

The crazy part is that I'd been thinking about asking her for over a month. But something always stopped me; I couldn't pull the trigger. It was never the right moment; something else always took over our conversations.

But sitting in silence in the ER, I knew that was the moment. Was it romantic? No. Was it the perfect scenario? No. Was it memorable? Yes.

And that's what we men want.

We want that unforgettable moment. We want to see that look of surprise. We want to make our ladies the happiest women on the planet.

Now, about those texts, they were also for us. I wanted to seal the deal. "Forsaking all others" started right then. Some of these women were remarkably close friends, so I wanted them to know personally that our friendship was changing. Not everyone needs to know about your engagement through "Facebook Official."

The responses varied greatly. Some were extremely excited that I'd found my wife-to-be. They asked for details, wanted to meet her, and some asked for invitations to the wedding. Some were indifferent to the news, with responses like "I'm glad to hear that" and "Congratulations to her."

Then there was the final group: the doubters. Their responses included, "Are you sure?" "I thought y'all were just friends," and "Are you really sure? Maybe you need to think about that."

Categorically speaking, the excited people were my real friends, the indifferent ones were candidates, and the doubters were close family and friends. But here's one thing to remember about responses: no one loves you more than your close friends and family. While their answers may catch you off guard, they come from a good place. So don't trip unless they get out of hand.

❧ 8 ❧

TILL DEATH?

Marriage isn't just the joining of a man and woman in the union of holy matrimony; it's the fusion of two separate lives into one cohesive unit. However, when you start blending lives replete with individual habits, divergent opinions, and unique preferences, the adjustment might feel more like a collision than a union.

Yet marriage is a commitment.

I adore married life—it's a beautiful thing. Choosing to forsake singledom, settle down with one woman, and share my existence with her for the rest of my life is a testament to the transformative power of marriage. I am committed to this one woman, no matter what happens.

Here's the crux: we both must be fully committed to each other—one man, one woman, period.

The cracks in our resolve often surface when our commitment faces trials. Tests of commitment aren't solely about covenant violations, such as cheating or adultery. We face trials in various forms. For a reason, traditional vows include the phrase, "for better, for worse, for richer, for poorer, in sickness and in health, to love and to cherish, till death do us part." Each scenario separated by a comma serves as a test of our commitment.

Like life itself, marriage is a roller coaster. You will confront all those "commas." We relish the positive ones: better, richer, health. But what transpires when we face the negatives: worse, poorer, sickness?

Take my parents' marriage, for example. They weathered all these commas, but one thing remained constant: my dad was steadfast till the very end. My mother passed away from lung cancer. Throughout her illness, and until her final moments, my father was ever-present. Remarkably, before succumbing to lung cancer, my mother had survived two distinct forms of breast cancer, prolonging her years of illness.

My father's test lay in whether he would continue supporting her despite his unease around hospitals, doctors, needles, and medical tubes. He passed that test with excellence.

Again, expect to face all these commas.

The key to overcoming such trials is setting ground rules and expectations for your marriage. Without expectations, you surrender control, reacting to life's vicissitudes instead of responding thoughtfully. You end up like a dinghy tossed around by ocean waves.

Personally, I aim to be a ship, purposefully navigating through the waves, moving toward a specific goal. And here are some suggestions on how to do that.

JACKIE SMITH, JR.

OTHER PEOPLE DON'T MATTER

When it comes to my marriage, the only person I aim to please is my wife. I firmly believe in the "Leave and Cleave" philosophy. The Bible states in Matthew 19:5 (KJV), *"For this cause shall a man leave father and mother, and shall cleave to his wife: and they twain shall be one flesh."*

While I remain my parents' son and wish to please them, they can no longer be my priority. I have taken a wife; she is now my primary focus. I cover her, and she covers me. She's the friend for whom I would lay down my life. This woman—my wife!

If I prioritize my wife over my parents, where does anyone else stand?

In this era of blurred values and misplaced priorities, our mistake often lies in allowing ourselves to be overwhelmed by an excess of "stuff," obscuring what's right and who's wrong. Social media bombard us with a range of images and thoughts, and news outlets inundate us with a continuous stream of negativity. There's no standard anymore; everyone's opinion seems to matter.

That shouldn't be the case. If you're not in my inner circle, you're irrelevant to me and my circle. While that might sound harsh, it's the truth.

We frequently become ensnared in debates about others' opinions on our domestic lives or parenting styles. I even rewrote the preface and the first two chapters of this book because of concerns over public perception and whether my words might be too abrasive for churchgoers. Yet, churchgoers make up one of the highest percentages of divorcees in the United States.

Our marriages often fail because we're overly concerned with others' opinions. Mary and Mark's thirty-year relationship doesn't grant Mary any right to advise my wife. Why? Because I'm not married to Mary; our lives and marriages are distinct.

Social media's accessibility is its curse. Posting about marital spats exposes the one you should be protecting. Public comments, when you've invited them, can be vexing.

Another arena where others don't matter is within blended families. When I married my first wife, she had a fifteen-year-old son, a seven-year-old daughter, and a three-month-old son. We became one family because I engaged purposefully with each member. I handled night-time cries and supported our daughter and oldest son in their needs. My wife took on the role of disciplinarian. We didn't let others invade our space, even when one of the biological fathers lived nearby.

My guiding principle is, "If they don't matter, they don't matter, period." So why discuss the irrelevant? This leads me to my next point.

LEAVE THE PAST IN THE PAST

When dealing with the past, men and women can differ significantly. To one spouse, the past might become irrelevant within less than five seconds, while the other may cling to the past as if it's still a part of the present.

Some of the most invaluable advice I ever received came from my stepmother. When she married Joe, he told her, "If you don't inquire about the past, I won't discuss it. I won't ask about your past, either. What matters is what we share right now." Remarkably, they never discussed people or events from their previous lives and enjoyed an extraordinary marriage.

Regrettably, I received this advice only after I'd got the "run-offs" with my fiancée. I had given her an overview of my previous life, believing that understanding my history would enable her to better comprehend my feelings and decisions. However, the issue was not that I was sharing, but that I failed to consider her capacity to process this information. I inundated her with names and details, unintentionally giving her reasons to dislike people she had never met. My past became fodder for disagreements, and she used it against me. In my attempt to be transparent, I unwittingly introduced negativity into her present and mine.

Here's what I learned: God designed us to

be givers, and couples should reciprocate that giving, even prioritizing the other's needs. Yet, what we share should build up each other. In my eagerness to be transparent, I failed to recognize that I was planting negative seeds rather than strengthening her as a partner.

The act of giving always involves receiving, and what is received is carried forward, whether it is constructive or not. Our words and actions have the power to strengthen or weaken others. For instance, if a man like Daniel is unfaithful to Margaret, he sows a seed of mistrust that will affect her future relationships. As a result, if I marry Margaret, I may have to contend with the trust issues Daniel instilled in her, possibly even needing to uproot a deeply entrenched tree of mistrust for our relationship to thrive.

Sharing is caring, but we must be judicious in what we share, how much we share, and how we share it. Some aspects of the past should remain there; they don't improve our present lives.

And that leads me to another thought.

❧

IF SOMETHING MATTERS TO THAT SPECIAL PERSON IN YOUR LIFE, THEN IT SHOULD MATTER TO YOU

Over the years, I've matured and developed a specific quality: emotional detachment toward things I don't care about. This is a development because, for many years, my emotional investment was disproportionately high in something that had no impact on my family or me.

A news event could unfold, and I'd be distraught. The Raiders losing another game would infuriate me. I was overly empathetic toward other people's problems. It got so bad that my wife once asked me if I was menstruating. Yes, it was that bad!

So, I learned to distance myself from situations that didn't directly affect me. The problem is, I'm analytical by nature. I pull away just enough to analyze a situation, which then morphs into unsolicited feedback. In a marriage, emotional detachment is not always the right approach, especially when my wife feels strongly about a situation.

Now, I'm speaking directly to the men. One of the worst things we can do is oversimplify a situation that our wives are going through. We've all been guilty of it.

Imagine coming home from work to find your wife upset. Your first thought is, "What did I do?" Then follows an investigative period that ranges from fifteen minutes to an hour, depending on the severity of the issue at hand. The bigger the problem, the longer the conversation and the apology—and possibly, the more lavish the make-up gift. However, focusing on the potential rewards may be premature. Sometimes gratification must be postponed.

Eventually, she reveals the issue: Johnny left his muddy shoes on the freshly cleaned carpet instead of in the mudroom.

You mentally check off:

- Awesome, it wasn't me.
- I'll talk to Johnny.
- Now, Mommy will be happy.

- Make-up time!

You then say, "Don't worry about it. I'll take care of it," thus stepping into a new realm of trouble. You've minimized the issue because it didn't matter to you—but it mattered to her.

The saying "Happy Wife, Happy Life" isn't about treating her like royalty. It's about acknowledging her concerns and prioritizing them accordingly.

Men seek peace and often look for the quickest route to it. Women want peace too, but they value respect more. By offering a curt response, you don't show respect for her feelings. What she needs to hear is your genuine concern, something beyond a dismissive "Don't worry about it."

Many men are reticent about expressing their feelings. Had you articulated your thoughts more thoroughly, you might have reached the make-up stage sooner. But by reducing your response to one-liners, she feels disrespected and not valued. Phase two of this episode will then shift to how you didn't grasp the gravity of the situation, questioning your respect for her.

It's a continual struggle to find this balance, but it's achievable. It just takes time.

Speaking of balance...

৩৯৫

TAKE PLENTY OF VACATIONS

I passionately believe in taking a break from our normal day-to-day operations, especially when we're married.

One of the most significant mistakes couples make is ignoring vacations. The average worker in the United States receives fifteen days of paid leave each year. However, a recent survey revealed that fifty-two percent of Americans did not use all their paid vacation days in 2017.

Did you know that in Austria, citizens receive thirty-eight mandatory paid days off, consisting of thirteen public holidays and twenty-five days of annual leave?

Did you know that the top ten reasons marriages fail all point to one central problem? Stress!

We are stressing each other out. Regardless of whether the problems are related to finances, communication, or general family issues, we acknowledge that time should be allotted for breaks.

When I say "vacation," I don't mean

booking a seven-day family package to Disney World or embarking on a ten-day cruise to some faraway land. According to Merriam-Webster, vacation is defined as (1) a period spent away from home or business in travel or recreation, and (2) a respite or time of respite from something.

In short, an intermission.

We need to take an intermission from our daily lives, whether it's something as simple as going to a local water park and renting an on-site room for the night, securing a cabin at one of your state's national parks for a weekend getaway, or taking a day trip to visit a winery. The key here is a departure from our regular routines.

For married people, I recommend taking at least three vacations each year.

The "Everybody" Vacation

As the name suggests, this vacation includes the whole family. Depending on the ages of your children, major amusement parks like Six Flags, Universal Studios, Cedar Point, or Disney World are options.

Amusement parks are designed with

family in mind, although the cost may be prohibitive. Some parks charge as much as seventy dollars per person just for admission, which doesn't include rides or food. An alternative would be local festivals and county or state fairs, where admission is more affordable, yet families can still enjoy rides and food.

National parks such as Yellowstone, the Grand Canyon, and Yosemite are awe-inspiring destinations. However, local metro or state reserve parks offer a cheaper way to appreciate nature's beauty.

Have you ever considered visiting another city, like Washington, D.C., Gatlinburg, or Ocean City? Or perhaps Myrtle Beach, the Outer Banks, or South Beach? These trips can offer diverse experiences for you and your family.

Being a history buff, I like to point out historical landmarks when traveling. This way, vacations offer a bit of educational value as well.

The "Our" Vacation

The second type of vacation that we should take is the "Our Vacation." We often reserve these vacations for special events such as anniversaries, birthdays, and other meaningful moments. But regardless of the reason, an "Our Vacation" is our time to disconnect from our jobs, homes, and families and enjoy each other's company.

All of the above destinations are fine, but this is when we need to shift into romantic gear. Let's embark on a three-day cruise to the Bahamas, indulge in a couples' massage, and relax in our room. Alternatively, let's book a suite at the Four Seasons downtown, lounge by the pool for a bit, and then order room service.

It's not about where you go or what you're doing. It's about relaxing. We confront life's challenges every day: the morning commute, work deadlines, and then the evening commute back home to cook, clean, and care for the children. And then we repeat the cycle the following day and the day after that.

So, when we go on "Our Vacation," the

objective is to disconnect. No phone calls home. Stay off Facebook and Instagram. Simply enjoy the company of the person to whom you've pledged your life and your love. Why? Because it's "Our Vacation."

The "My" Vacation

The third type of vacation is the "My Vacation." Just because you're married doesn't mean you have to be in each other's company constantly. Women need time with other women, and the same holds true for men.

Some of the best vacations I've had while married were the ones I took without my spouse and children. Sometimes, I went alone; at other times, I joined or met up with some of my guy friends.

The shortest "My Vacation" I ever took lasted approximately four and a half hours. I left home and went to my church for a men-only event. We watched the Super Bowl on big screens, ordered food from Hooters, and ate directly from the trays. Hardly anyone used napkins. There was a lot of joking, burping, and laughing—pure goofing off.

One comment I frequently heard was, "If

my wife saw me doing this..." It was a memorable time that I'll never forget.

Regardless of the type of vacation you choose—whether it's an "Everybody Vacation," an "Our Vacation," or a "My Vacation"—take one. Vacations are healing.

❧ 9 ❧
DEATH

How do you transition from the joy, excitement, and exhilaration of vacationing to the subject of death? For readers, a smooth transition from one topic to another is ideal. But, alas, death plays by no one's rules.

It's like a game of "Hide and Seek." Death has covered its eyes and is counting down. Once the count ends—ready or not — here it comes.

So, here we are.

Earlier, we discussed the concept that *"He that findeth a wife findeth a good thing"* (Proverbs

18:22, KJV). While that may be true, all things, even good ones, must come to an end.

The Three Ds: Death, Divorce, and Desertion

All marriages, like any other relationships, eventually end. In this chapter, we focus on the one termination over which we have no control: death. Whether your marriage is good, bad, or something in between, death will eventually knock on your door.

Hebrews 9:27 (KJV) states, *"...it is appointed unto men once to die..."* It's inescapable. This is one appointment that will not be missed.

When a loved one dies, those who remain experience grief.

I remember when my mother passed away. Watching her take her final breath was one of the most horrifying events of my life. My calmness was eerie; I was in a trance. I couldn't believe it had happened.

Whether we called 911 or hospice is a blur. But what I vividly recall is the gentle care they took with her body. They moved her from the bed to the gurney with the utmost respect.

Her face remained uncovered until they placed her in the back of the hearse.

Chasing after the hearse as it drove away, I was finally broken when the car turned the corner.

Children in a marriage are affected perhaps as much, or even more, than the husband and wife. Why? Because we are a family. We are married. We are all part of this union.

The Loss

Losing a spouse is a harsh transition. You lose your life partner, your "better half," your best friend, and your closest confidant—all simultaneously. Your life seems to grind to a halt, and the idea of moving on initially feels almost disrespectful to the one who has passed.

Every loss brings grief, but losing a spouse brings anguish, one of the most challenging experiences to navigate. Attempting to avoid the grieving process only hinders the healing that you need. With each of the Three Ds, loss and inevitable grief occur.

THE FIVE STAGES OF GRIEF

Understanding the Five Stages of Grief—how to recognize them and how to respond—is vital. This applies both to the grieving individual and those who are trying to help. The grieving process is both real and intensely personal, whether you're seven or seventy.

❧

DENIAL

When I chased that car down the street, I was in denial. I couldn't believe my mom was dead. I didn't want to believe it; I couldn't stand the thought that she was gone. When we are in denial, we neglect or deny the truth. We try to get a handle on life but can't make heads or tails of what's happening to us.

Our minds are filled with a billion questions: Why her? Or "Why him?" "Why now?" "How am I going to make it alone?"

Children wonder what their father or mother will do next. "What about my brother? My sister?"

Often, those who are left behind start thinking things like, "Maybe she's not really dead," or, "Maybe someone didn't check her pulse correctly," or, "He'll wake up, and everything will be okay, the way it's supposed to be."

And then there's the denial that keeps saying, "This isn't real; maybe we're just in a bad episode of *The Twilight Zone*."

Denial, in whatever form, is a coping mechanism to make the current situation more bearable. It is a natural and temporary step in the process.

My only concern with denial is when it isn't temporary. We must move forward through grief and not let it become a lifestyle.

Being stuck is unhealthy. Living in grief will affect every aspect of your life. I know a guy who genuinely relives the emotions of death every time he passes a specific restaurant, hears a song on the radio, or engages in conversations about the deceased.

When we recognize people aren't moving on, we need to assist them in getting help.

❧

ANGER

The next stage in the grieving process is anger.

My world was crushed in more ways than one. Not only did I grapple with the denial questions, but I also questioned my faith.

I was angry with God! How could He take her? Why didn't He heal her just as He did all those other times? Why did He let those other people live? She was far better than they were, but they're still here.

I served my church, but my heart was on fire. I played the organ every Sunday, yet my spirit was elsewhere. I ministered in song and even preached to the people, but the message was blocked from my heart because of my anger toward God.

This is where support plays a crucial role. Unchecked anger will continue to grow and fester. People do crazy things when they're angry. Some even black out and don't remember their actions or words due to anger. Therefore, if you are part of a community and recognize that someone is struggling with this anger, please be present for them. Make your presence felt.

I have a friend who randomly sends me encouraging emails and text messages. She's been doing this for over twenty years. Why? Because, at one time, I sent her encouraging and uplifting emails. My messages helped her so much that she turned around and began doing it herself.

Interestingly, I don't always read the messages the moment they're sent. It may be hours or even days later. But when I read them, they are helpful at that very moment!

❧

BARGAINING

Whether occurring before or after death, bargaining is real. This is where we negotiate with God, and all the "what if" questions flow. "What if I started paying my tithes correctly? What if I started driving homeless people to their appointments? What if I...? What if I...?"

The good thing about bargaining is that at least we're moving on from anger, and even those around us can notice a change. But many of our thoughts and ideas are irrational.

This is where guilt rears its head. Phrases like "If I would have...," "If I could have...," and "If only..." become staples in our conversations.

We've come to grips with the fact that the loss is real. But we're searching for ways we could have fixed things. "Once I pay penance for whatever, I'll wake up tomorrow, and things will return to *normal*." But tomorrow never comes.

It's my fault they died because I wore my white sneakers after Labor Day. If only I could go back and wear my Timbs, then I might have prevented it from happening. And then there's self-blame: "If I had been a better person, God would not have taken them."

As supporters, we must understand that the person is in a time warp. The death may have occurred forty years ago, but this person is still there. They've been trying to negotiate the best deal with fate, but fate isn't cooperating. Understanding and concern are essential traits to possess. The person also needs occasional reality checks.

࿐

DEPRESSION

When we realize that our bargaining isn't working, the emotion of the situation returns vigorously. And here comes depression.

Depression is that sense of hopelessness, abandonment, and total emptiness. Nothing you say or do matters. Food loses its taste, and everything is blah. You're trapped in the prison of your mind and feelings. The only reality you experience is the bubble of numbness you inhabit.

I'm keeping these stages brief because I'm reliving some challenging times in my life, even as I type.

Here's some real talk: I was diagnosed with situational depression over ten years after my mom passed away. I thought I was doing okay. I was married with children and had a pretty good job. Bills were getting paid.

But a particular scenario played out in my life, revealing that I was still mourning my mom. I was literally curled up on my couch. I didn't want to eat or hang out with my children; I wanted nothing to do with life.

But I sought help. I spent the next four years in counseling. It's not an overnight success sort of thing; it takes time. Think of it like weight loss: if it took several years for you to gain the weight, would it be reasonable to expect to lose it in a week?

The role of support at this stage is availability, listening, and finally, asking relevant questions: "You have counseling today. What time are you going?" "Did you go to counseling today?" "How was your visit?" "Did you learn anything new?" "Is there anything you'd like to share?"

Don't badger the person. Just ask general questions and listen to the responses. One of the most aggravating things is answering a question only to have the person ask it again —or worse, getting the details wrong, indicating they weren't listening and didn't really care.

Case in point: my counselor's name was Casey. When I first started seeing her, I went twice a week for nearly a year. So, Casey was a significant person in my life. If you were part of my support team and I'd been seeing a counselor for almost two years, why wouldn't you know who Casey is?

Depression is no joke and should not be taken lightly. At this stage, love is the most essential tool you have at your disposal. When I can feel your love and care, it helps break the hold depression has on me. Add that to the tools I'm receiving from my counselor, and things will move in the right direction.

❧

ACCEPTANCE

Acceptance, as defined by Merriam-Webster, is "the act of accepting something or someone; the fact of being accepted." Note that nowhere in this definition does it state that acceptance means everything is okay.

Acceptance signifies acknowledging that "it is what it is," and there's nothing I can do about it. To this day, when I think about certain loved ones who have passed away, I cry. The emotions are overwhelming; I feel a pounding in my chest and grieve all over again.

The "Five Stages of Grief" is not akin to running a four-hundred-meter dash. You don't merely begin at the starting line and run until you cross the finish line. No, we oscillate within this healing process, sometimes even between stages. You may have crossed off denial and anger but find yourself reverting to denial while bargaining. The process starts anew.

So, even though I've reached acceptance, it doesn't mean the grieving is "over." As part of a support team, your goal should be to be there for one another as needed.

10

THE SECOND OF THE THREE DS: DIVORCE

U nlike death, divorce is a decision made by at least one party. Divorce is difficult because it declares that, for whatever reason or reasons, the marriage is not worth saving, maintaining, or fighting for.

I'm no angel—I've never claimed to be. I wasn't born with angel wings already attached. I accept full responsibility for my part in the failure of my two marriages. However, neither were my ex-wives angels.

A common misconception many people hold is that the other individual must be a terrible person. Well, I can't subscribe to that view, and if you are a divorcee and honest with yourself, your ex probably wasn't that bad either. Exceptions exist, of course, such as cases involving abuse or addiction.

My ex-wives were beautiful, strong, independent, intelligent, and loving women. At one point, we failed the "for worse" test.

MARRIAGE: MORE THAN A SOCIAL CONTRACT

Marriage is an incredible institution! Out of my forty-seven years of life, I've been married for nearly twenty-three. To say that marriage is all sunshine and daisies would be a bald-faced lie.

Marriage is HARD. It's an adjustment of two lives with the mutual intent of blending, although sometimes it feels more like a collision than a merger.

The Ultimate Social Experiment

We're akin to lab rats in the experiment of marriage. The first part of our lives is spent under our parents' guidance, adhering to specific rules for our safety and development. At a certain point, we wish to establish our rules.

So, we strike out on our own, living "perfect" lives—until we meet that special someone. Now, we must reset our rules because we're no longer single individuals: we're a couple.

Although we've exchanged vows before God and witnesses, we're not truly prepared for marriage until we recognize that our previous rules are no longer applicable. Both parties must create new rules together. That moment marks genuine maturity and readiness for a successful marriage.

The Complexity of Life

Life, however, isn't that simple. For some, rules are meant to be broken. Poor decisions can lead to an unharmonious union.

I've been unfaithful and engaged in extramarital relationships, which led to the demise of our marriage. Even when this betrayal came to light, we stayed married and pick up the pieces—at least, that was the plan.

Fellas, when we breach trust with our

wives, we've damaged the most critical aspect of our relationship. Women will tolerate a lack of money if your hustle is solid. Men are no different. Infidelity is painful for everyone involved. In fact, we men might even handle it worse than women.

I had a girlfriend whom I deeply loved, and she cheated on me. What compounded the pain was that I knew the guy involved. I felt shattered and didn't want to talk or be around her. I insisted she get medical tests, and even after she received an "all clear," I still couldn't bear to be with her—despite loving her.

Imagine experiencing such betrayal with someone you live with, someone to whom you've committed your life. That, I believe, is the ultimate test of "for worse."

When life's complexities arise, decisions must be made. Do we stay together and attempt to mend what's broken? Do we separate and try to move on? Or do we work on resolving issues even if we've opted for separate lives? The imperative to fix the relationship remains; otherwise, we risk repeating the same mistakes.

There's no room for dilly-dallying; resolve the issues as they appear to avoid a pile-up of problems that will eventually doom the marriage.

What Are Marriage Killers?

According to a September 18, 2018, article by Shellie Warren on Marriage.com, the ten most common reasons for divorce are:

1. Infidelity
2. Money
3. Lack of Communication
4. Constant Arguing
5. Weight Gain
6. Unrealistic Expectations
7. Lack of Intimacy
8. Lack of Equality
9. Unpreparedness for Marriage
10. Abuse

For more information, I suggest visiting Marriage.com.

How to Fix It

Your marriage isn't over until it's over. Several effective methods can save a marriage, but the linchpin is personal responsibility and diligent effort.

First and foremost, God needs to be at the center of your marriage. Without divine guidance, we can accomplish nothing. Prayer, attending services, and faith-based counseling for both partners are crucial steps to healing.

For further guidance, consider self-help books like "The Love Dare" by Eric Wilson. Initially, a devotional for one partner, the book has evolved into a series beneficial for couples and families alike.

Don't let problems fester. Your marriage is too valuable to be abandoned or neglected.

So, here are Seven Strong Steps to Stop a Divorce, according to Susan Heitler, Ph.D., as written for Psychology Today.[1]

1. Prepare for Action

Don't let it ride. Failing to plan is planning to fail. Create an action plan to save your marriage.

2. Smother the Urge to Play the Victim

Skip the "poor me" and switch to "proud me." There are a myriad of reasons you are married. Remind yourself of your outstanding qualities. Be the vibrant, enjoyable person you truly are. Don't boast about your efforts; let your actions speak for themselves.

3. Clarify What You Need to Change

We often tell our spouses what we dislike about them. Create a list of these points, share it with your spouse for verification, and then embark on a personal journey to identify the roots of these behaviors. Your upbringing —whether in a two-parent or single-parent home—could influence your actions. Once realized, work to fix these foundational issues.

4. Look Your Best

When vying for someone's affection, we go the extra mile. Apply the same effort in saving your marriage. Ladies, apply a little makeup; men, groom yourselves. A few new outfits can refresh your appearance and boost your self-esteem.

5. Clean Up Old Hurts

This step isn't easy. Create a list of marital hurts, angers, and resentments with your spouse. Go through each item to identify mistakes, miscommunications, and misunderstandings. Apologize and plan to do better in the future.

6. Believe in Yourself

Self-love is key. If you want your spouse to love you, you must first love yourself. For those who struggle with this, Dr. Heitler recommends a technique called "temporal tapping" to aid in reprogramming your mindset.

7. Learn Essential Skills for Marriage

Marriage isn't about perfection; it's about working with our individual flaws. Unfortunately, there's no college course titled "Marriage 101." We learn by trial and error. Now that you're aware of these skills, you have two options: ignore them or start the learning process.

Divorce doesn't have to be the inevitable outcome, though it may unfortunately be the end result for some.

Things to Think About

Sometimes divorce will occur, irrespective of the number of tools we employ, counselors we consult, flowers we send, or conversations we engage in.

I grappled with these elements, and the harder I tried to salvage our marriage, the more difficulties arose.

One day, while visiting my brother John, I found myself tearful over my marital woes. John listened patiently as I poured out my concerns.

After listening for about thirty minutes, John posed a series of questions.

John: Does God show favoritism?
Me: (I knew John was referring to Romans 2:11, which in the King James Version states, "For there is no respect of persons with God.") So, I replied, "No."
John: Whom does God answer when two people pray for different outcomes in the same situation?
Me: He answers neither, as He shows no favoritism.
John: Have you ever considered that

perhaps you and your wife are not
praying for the same thing?
Me: [Stunned silence]

The thought had never crossed my mind
that our marriage might be beyond repair. I
spent the next several days contemplating that
last question.

Eventually, my wife and I had a crucial
conversation and agreed that it was best to
proceed separately. Nevertheless, it was a long
and challenging journey.

My Advice

If you and your spouse can resolve matters
without attorneys, then do so. Coming to an
agreement and filing for a dissolution of
marriage is much simpler than undergoing a
divorce.

The key to either dissolving or divorcing
lies in reaching an agreement. There will be
give-and-take from both parties. If one person
opts only to take, the process becomes
lengthy and costly. This process can consume
both parties; not only will your marriage end,

but your livelihood could be severely compromised as well.

If children are involved in the divorce, don't place them in the middle. They aren't playing cards, sources of income, or tools for vengeance against the other parent. They are the future.

Our children adopt behaviors from us. So, men, treat your women properly, even if they are currently challenging. And women, treat your men with respect—perhaps even more than they deserve. As your children observe, you shape their understanding of how to behave and react as adults. Do them and yourselves a favor: demonstrate grace and civility, even when disagreements make life challenging.

If both of you are at each other's throats during this process, your children will take sides, which benefits no one.

As a father, I fought for my children and had custody of them. Men, if you want your children, fight for them. Don't automatically assume that the court will award custody to the mother, leaving you paying child support for the next eighteen years.

Conclusion

Although our marriages may fail, we are not failures. You loved this woman; you married her; you had children with her. There's no reason you can't maintain a cordial —if not friendly—relationship, especially when children are involved.

Divorce doesn't signify the end of life with that person. That individual remains your children's mother or father, with an ongoing role in their lives. You have a duty to instill respect for the other parent in your children.

DESERTION: THE FINAL "D"

The last of the Three Ds is desertion, alternatively termed abandonment, dereliction, or forsaking. Regardless of the label or form, there are two primary reasons desertion is invoked to end a marriage: safety and cowardice.

Safety First

If a person's safety is at risk, exiting the relationship by any means necessary is imperative. There is never a justification for domestic abuse. The instant violence enters the equation; the marriage should be considered over. This doesn't mean arguments, disagreements, or heated conversations won't occur; I'm specifically addressing physical and mental abuse. According to Wikipedia, physical abuse is "any intentional act causing injury or trauma to another person."

Changing Gender Dynamics in Abuse

In days past, the focus was often on men who raised their hands to women. However, today's reality shows a rising number of victimized men. Regrettably, men generally don't report abuse, fearing it will diminish their perceived masculinity. Let me clarify unequivocally: any form of domestic abuse is unacceptable, regardless of who commits it or in what form it manifests.

Personal Lessons on Handling Conflict

My parents taught me the mantra, "Be the man." That means when a situation becomes volatile, I walk away. I've learned that when things escalate, it's prudent to call the police. I am no less a man for doing so.

In one of my relationships, a heated

conversation turned dangerous when a glass jar full of coins was hurled at me as I descended the stairs. The jar shattered above my head, raining down change and shards of glass. While angry, I exercised restraint. Retaliating would have only worsened the situation and likely resulted in my arrest. Instead, I dialed 911.

A Call to Men: Protect Yourself

By the time law enforcement arrived, the atmosphere had calmed significantly. My partner had started cleaning up, and I met the officers at the door. From this experience, I learned men should not hesitate to contact the authorities; we are not automatically assumed to be the aggressors. Police are there for our protection, just as they are for women.

But immediate change is imperative when either person feels that their only recourse is more abuse. I know individuals who have been assaulted with baseball bats, frying pans, and television remotes. Their spouses have even hospitalized some. I know a woman who fired a gun at her daughter's boyfriend. These incidents are not mere stories; they are happening. When your life is at stake, leave.

In some situations, departure under cover of darkness may be advisable for your safety. Lingering for a conversation about divorce might only exacerbate the situation.

Cowardice as Another Form of Desertion

The other cause of desertion is cowardice. As previously mentioned, marriage is work. Like any job, there will be times when you don't feel like working. That doesn't mean you should quit.

Consider a couple experiencing marital difficulties. They argued, but divorce was never part of their dialogue. One evening, the husband left for a midweek church service at seven o'clock while his under-the-weather wife stayed home. He returned at nine o'clock to discover she had moved out. In less than two and a half hours, she had emptied the house of all her belongings. And when I say, "her belongings," I mean she took everything she had ever purchased during their marriage—right down to the carpet padding and wall plates for light switches and electrical outlets.

In another example, a couple couldn't come to a final agreement on their divorce. After six months of negotiation, the wife planned a weekend getaway with their children—only she had no intention of returning. She had already filed for divorce a month prior and updated her address with the court the day before her departure.

These actions represent forms of cowardice. Neither party was willing to have the tough conversations necessary for a graceful exit. From the outside looking in, these men were not violent, so abuse was not the issue. The crux of the problem was the immaturity of all parties involved.

There comes a time when men must "put on your big-boy pants," and women must "put on their big-girl panties." Even if the conversation is awkward, if you need to leave, that's your prerogative. But avoiding the conversation is a sign of immaturity, irrespective of age.

Fortunately, the men in these scenarios

had robust support systems, which isn't the case for everyone. Desertion is unnecessary when there's no threat of abuse. If the marriage is faltering, talk it out and find an equitable solution—don't just walk away.

❧ 12 ❧

EMBRACING SINGLEHOOD AGAIN

No matter which of the "Three Ds" brought your marriage to an end—divorce, death, or desertion—the result is the same: you're single again. The upside is that you now have memories, experiences, and a wealth of new perspectives about relationships.

The lives we build with our spouses position us differently from our earlier single days. You may have accumulated capital, established a home, or even have children. These factors influence your thoughts about the future, heightening your awareness of life and responsibilities. The familiar saying "To whom much is given, much is required" holds true, especially concerning insight.

Self-Reflection and Life's Cycle

When I found myself single again, significant factors differentiated my current state from my past: I had children, a mortgage to manage, and a career to navigate. Moreover, I had to think intensively and frequently about my identity.

We must consider who we are today versus who we thought we were in our earlier years. Decisions we made twenty years ago aren't necessarily the choices we'd make today. Our viewpoints have evolved because of our experiences, warranting self-examination to be truly honest with ourselves.

At this life stage, we should revisit this book's starting point: healing from the Three Ds and rediscovering single satisfaction. We need to identify our present selves and determine our current desires.

Life may seem like an ever-forward journey, but it can also resemble a giant wheel. Although you might find yourself in familiar situations, those points offer new perspectives —indicative of your life's momentum.

Personal Anecdote: A Love Story Full Circle

I met my wife over thirty years ago, and she was outstanding. However, my shyness led me to love her from a distance. We sang together in a community gospel choir. Life circumstances kept us apart—births, other relationships, and even my stint in the United States Air Force. Despite these separations, I never missed sending her birthday wishes because we were friends.

Life has a way of bringing us full circle. After my divorce, when I had attained "single and satisfied" status and clarified what I wanted, I reconnected with the woman who would become my wife.

The Choice to Remain Single

However, it's worth noting that some people opt to stay single after marriage; there's nothing wrong with that. My grandfather, for example, lived over twenty years after my grandmother's passing, genuinely single and satisfied. Family and a supportive community surrounded him, and he lived life on his terms.

In Closing

Life is worth living, and regardless of the path you choose, prioritize your relationship with God. Believe that your future will be brighter than your past.

I pray this book assists you in reaching that brighter future. If you haven't yet established a relationship with God, you should. Repeat this prayer to begin your spiritual journey:

"Dear Lord, I am a sinner. Please forgive me of my sins. I believe you sent your son, Jesus, to die for my sins and that he was raised from the dead. I invite you into my heart. From today forward, my life is yours. Thank you for your saving grace."

If you genuinely believe, then you are saved. Find a Bible-believing church and deepen your relationship with Jesus.

The Holy Spirit is a gift—believe it and receive it.

I love you all!

ENDNOTES

2. WHO ARE YOU

1. https://www.simplypsychology.org/maslow.html

10. THE SECOND OF THE THREE DS: DIVORCE

1. Psychology Today: 7 Strong Steps to Stop a Divorce

ABOUT THE AUTHOR

Jackie Smith, Jr. is an African-American writer who grew up in Columbus, Ohio. Using his experiences as a technical trainer, business owner, professional musician, and licensed minister he penned, Establishing Glory, a faith-based self-help series.

His goal in life is to help people be their best which he does it by shining an unfiltered light on the challenges of his own life including faith, marriage, music, divorce, and parenting in the 2000s.

facebook.com/MrJMerrill

twitter.com/MrJMerrill

instagram.com/MrJMerrill

ALSO BY JACKIE SMITH, JR.

Establishing Glory: The Praise and Worship
Handbook (ISBN: 9781950719006)

www.ingramcontent.com/pod-product-compliance
Lightning Source LLC
Chambersburg PA
CBHW031129020426
42333CB00012B/300